Collins English

Amazing Entrepreneurs and Business People

Level 1
CEF A2

Text by
Helen Parker

Series edited by
Fiona MacKenzie

Collins

HarperCollins Publishers
77–85 Fulham Palace Road
Hammersmith London W6 8JB

10 9 8 7 6 5 4 3 2 1

Original text
© The Amazing People Club Ltd

Adapted text
© HarperCollins Publishers Ltd 2014

ISBN: 978-0-00-754501-8

Collins® is a registered trademark of HarperCollins Publishers Limited

www.collinselt.com

A catalogue record for this book is available from the British Library

Printed in the UK by Martins the Printers

All rights reserved. No part of this book may be reproduced, stored in a retrieval system, or transmitted in any form or by any means, electronic, mechanical, photocopying, recording or otherwise, without the prior permission in writing of the Publisher. This book is sold subject to the conditions that it shall not, by way of trade or otherwise, be lent, re-sold, hired out or otherwise circulated without the Publisher's prior consent in any form of binding or cover other than that in which it is published and without a similar condition including this condition being imposed on the subsequent purchaser.

HarperCollins does not warrant that www.collinselt.com or any other website mentioned in this title will be provided uninterrupted, that any website will be error free, that defects will be corrected, or that the website or the server that makes it available are free of viruses or bugs. For full terms and conditions please refer to the site terms provided on the website.

These readers are based on original texts (BioViews®) published by The Amazing People Club group.® BioViews® and The Amazing People Club® are registered trademarks and represent the views of the author.

BioViews® are scripted virtual interview based on research about a person's life and times. As in any story, the words are only an interpretation of what the individuals mentioned in the BioViews® could have said. Although the interpretations are based on available research, they do not purport to represent the actual views of the people mentioned. The interpretations are made in good faith, recognizing that other interpretations could also be made. The author and publisher disclaim any responsibility from any action that readers take regarding the BioViews® for educational or other purposes. Any use of the BioViews® materials is the sole responsibility of the reader and should be supported by their own independent research.

Cover image © Timof/Shutterstock

MIX
Paper from responsible sources
FSC
www.fsc.org
FSC™ C007454

FSC™ is a non-profit international organisation established to promote the responsible management of the world's forests. Products carrying the FSC label are independently certified to assure consumers that they come from forests that are managed to meet the social, economic and ecological needs of present and future generations, and other controlled sources.

Find out more about HarperCollins and the environment at
www.harpercollins.co.uk/green

♦ Contents ♦

Introduction	4
Mayer Amschel Rothschild	7
Cornelius Vanderbilt	15
W. K. Kellogg	25
Elizabeth Arden	33
Walt Disney	41
Soichiro Honda	51
Glossary	60

◆ INTRODUCTION ◆

Collins Amazing People Readers are collections of short stories. Each book presents the life story of five or six people whose lives and achievements have made a difference to our world today. The stories are carefully graded to ensure that you, the reader, will both enjoy and benefit from your reading experience.

You can choose to enjoy the book from start to finish or to dip into your favourite story straight away. Each story is entirely independent.

After every story a short timeline brings together the most important events in each person's life into one short report. The timeline is a useful tool for revision purposes.

Words which are above the required reading level are underlined the first time they appear in each story. All underlined words are defined in the glossary at the back of the book. Levels 1 and 2 take their definitions from the *Collins COBUILD Essential English Dictionary* and levels 3 and 4 from the *Collins COBUILD Advanced English Dictionary*.

To support both teachers and learners, additional materials are available online at www.collinselt.com/readers.

The Amazing People Club®

Collins Amazing People Readers are adaptations of original texts published by The Amazing People Club. The Amazing People Club is an educational publishing house. It was founded in 2006 by educational psychologist and management leader Dr Charles Margerison and publishes books, eBooks, audio books, iBooks and video content, which bring readers 'face to face' with many of the world's most inspiring and influential characters from the fields of art, science, music, politics, medicine and business.

♦ The Grading Scheme ♦

The Collins COBUILD Grading Scheme has been created using the most up-to-date language usage information available today. Each level is guided by a brand new comprehensive grammar and vocabulary framework, ensuring that the series will perfectly match readers' abilities.

		CEF band	Pages	Word count	Headwords
Level 1	elementary	A2	64	5,000–8,000	approx. 700
Level 2	pre-intermediate	A2–B1	80	8,000–11,000	approx. 900
Level 3	intermediate	B1	96	11,000–15,000	approx. 1,100
Level 4	upper intermediate	B2	112	15,000–19,000	approx. 1,700

For more information on the Collins COBUILD Grading Scheme, including a full list of the grammar structures found at each level, go to www.collinselt.com/readers/gradingscheme.

Also available online: Make sure that you are reading at the right level by checking your level on our website (www.collinselt.com/readers/levelcheck).

Mayer Amschel Rothschild
♦ ♦ ♦
1744–1812
the man who started one of the
richest banks in history

I came from a poor family but worked hard to build one of the biggest <u>fortunes</u> in history. I became the <u>banker</u> for many rich and <u>powerful</u> people. My sons, who also became <u>successful</u> bankers, <u>expanded</u> my business.

♦ ♦ ♦

I was born in a poor area of Frankfurt in Hesse (now part of Germany). I had seven brothers and sisters and my family never had enough money. My father had a small business. He bought and sold goods and did some <u>currency exchange</u>. I worked hard to help my family. I did jobs for my father and I learned a lot about his business. I learned how to buy and sell at the best price.

My father wanted me to learn to read and write. He also wanted me to learn useful business skills. So, in

1757, I was sent to Hanover to train with Jacob Wolf Oppenheimer, a banker.

♦ ♦ ♦

In Hanover, I learned all about banking. I was a quick learner and very good at mathematics. I learned that it wasn't enough to keep money in the bank. You also needed to use money and make good investments. I listened to the bank's richest clients. They knew many interesting ways to become rich.

The bank also owned a lot of rare coins and I became very interested in them. When I returned to Frankfurt, I started to buy and sell rare coins.

Soon my business was doing well and Prince William of Hesse became my client. The prince introduced me to many of his rich and powerful friends and they became clients, too.

♦ ◆ ♦

In 1785, the prince became King William the Ninth of Hesse. He and his friends often asked for my advice about money. They paid me well to make good investments for them. I often went to other countries and found the best investments. I <u>took</u> many <u>risks</u>, but I did well. I made a lot of money for my clients and myself. In this way, I became the international banker for many powerful people.

By that time, I had a wife and children. I married Guttle Schnapper in 1770, and we had ten children – five boys and five girls. I <u>trained</u> my boys in the business when they were very young. For our family, banking was more than a job. It was our family fortune and we had to protect it.

♦ ◆ ♦

I could see that the world was changing and I discovered many new <u>opportunities</u> for our business. The United States of America was <u>created</u> in 1776. It was a new country and it needed a national bank. In 1791, I became the main <u>shareholder</u> in the Bank of the United States. And, in 1804, when Napoleon Bonaparte became <u>Emperor</u> of France, many European governments were frightened. Napoleon wanted to <u>expand</u> his <u>empire</u> and rule other countries. These governments borrowed a lot of money from me to pay for soldiers to fight against Napoleon.

For our family, business was a kind of war. We always needed to protect ourselves and find new opportunities. My sons, who were now well trained, helped me to expand the Rothschild empire.

My eldest son, Amschel, became the head of our business in Frankfurt. He also became the head of the Rothschild empire when I died. My second son, Salomon, started a bank in Vienna, Austria. The government borrowed a lot of money from our bank to build the first railways in Austria.

Nathan, my third son, went to Manchester in England in 1798. At first, he started a company, which bought and sold goods. Then, in 1811, he opened our bank in London and made a fortune from gold and currency exchange.

My other two sons also started banks. Carl, my fourth son, started a banking business in Naples in Italy. And my fifth son, James opened our banking business in Paris, France, in 1812.

We borrowed and lent money to other companies and governments. We bought and sold gold and other valuable metals. We made it easier for countries to sell goods and services to each other. And our business grew and grew. It became one of the richest and most powerful banks in history.

We did everything we could to protect our fortune. We kept our money within our family and we invested in land and fine houses. I was one of the richest men in the world, but I was always afraid. Governments could change and we could lose our fortune at any time. At the end of my life in 1812, I asked myself the question, 'Will the Rothschild empire survive?'

The Life of Mayer Amschel Rothschild

1744   Mayer Amschel Rothschild was born in the city of Frankfurt in Hesse. He was the fourth of eight children. He helped his father in his small business.

1757   He started to train with Jacob Wolf Oppenheimer, who owned a bank in Hanover.

1763   Mayer returned to Frankfurt and started his own business. He bought and sold rare coins.

1769   Prince William of Hesse became a client. He introduced many important clients to Mayer's business.

1770   Mayer married Guttle Schnapper. They later had five sons and five daughters.

1773   Their first son, Amschel, was born. He later became the head of the Rothschild empire after Mayer died.

1774   Salomon, their second son, was born. In 1820, he started the family business in Vienna, Austria.

1777   The third son, Nathan, was born. In 1798, he started a business in Manchester, England. In 1811, he started the family's banking business in London, England.

1785 Prince William of Hesse became King William the Ninth. Mayer became the banker for the King and many of his friends.

1788 Mayer's fourth son, Carl, was born. In 1821 he moved to Naples in Italy and started the family's banking business there.

1791 Mayer became the biggest shareholder in the new Bank of the United States.

1792 His fifth son, James, was born. In 1812, he started the family business in Paris, France.

1804 Many European governments borrowed money from the Rothschilds to pay for wars against Napoleon.

1812 Mayer died in Frankfurt. He was 68 years old. His sons continued to expand the Rothschild empire.

Cornelius Vanderbilt

• ♦ •

1794–1877

the man who became one of the
richest people in the USA

My first success in business was with <u>ferries</u> and <u>steamships</u>. I bought many <u>lines</u> and opened new ones. I then did the same with railways. I became one of the richest businessmen in the history of the USA.

♦ ♦ ♦

My family came from the Netherlands to New York, USA, in 1650. I was born on Staten Island, which is close to Manhattan, the main island of New York City. I left school when I was 11 years old. I went to work with my father, who had his own ferry business between Staten Island and Manhattan. I collected money from passengers and did other small jobs.

In 1810, when I was 16 years old, I bought my own sailing boat and started my own ferry. I took passengers and goods between Staten Island and Manhattan. In 1812, a war started between the USA and the British. During the war, the army used my ferry to deliver goods along the Hudson River. I made enough money to get married and start a family.

In 1813, I married Sophia Johnson. We were together for 55 years and had 13 children. I had to work hard for my family. I continued with my own ferry business and worked with other companies, too. In 1817, Tom Gibbons asked me to be the captain of his steamship and then his business manager. I had to learn quickly so I watched and I listened. I learned that the most important thing in business is to make good decisions.

In 1818, when I was 24, I decided to <u>expand</u> our business. Aaron Ogden owned the only steamship company that could work on the Hudson River. I wanted to stop this <u>monopoly</u>. In 1824, in an important <u>legal case</u>, we won the <u>right</u> to start a steamship business along the Hudson River. When Tom Gibbons died in 1826, I worked for his son for a few years. Then I bought his business and opened several new ferry <u>services</u>, too.

In 1834, I tried to stop another monopoly – a steamship line between New York City and Albany. I started The People's Line to <u>compete</u> with this monopoly. In the end, my <u>competitors</u> paid me a lot of money to close The People's Line. I was happy because now I had the money to <u>invest</u> in some exciting new <u>opportunities</u>.

• ◆ •

In the 1830s, many factories were built in the New York area. The factory owners needed to deliver goods to other parts of the country and abroad. And the workers needed to travel longer distances from home to their work. It was also a time when many people were leaving Europe. These people wanted to move to the USA and to find new opportunities. And they all needed cheaper, faster transport to travel to the USA and within the country.

I decided to invest in railways and new steamship lines. And when the Gold Rush started in California in 1849, I was ready. I had the fastest (and cheapest!) trains and ships to take the gold back to New York City.

After a trip to Europe with my family in my steamship, *The North Star*, I decided to start a steamship business across the Atlantic. My biggest competitors were the Cunard Line and the Collins Line. I had the fastest ships and the lowest prices. Cunard and Collins couldn't compete with me and they had to close their lines.

• ◆ •

In 1861, the American Civil War started. The Unionists from the north of the country were fighting against the Confederates from the south of the country. I gave my biggest ship, *The Vanderbilt*, to the Unionists. I sold or lent them most of my other ships, too. Trains were becoming more and more popular, so I decided to expand my railway business.

In 1862, I bought the New York and Harlem Railroad. In 1864, I bought the Hudson River Railroad. And in 1867, I bought the New York Central Railroad. I asked my oldest son, Billy, to manage the Staten Island Railroad, which I started in 1851. Billy did a wonderful job and I asked him to manage all of my railway <u>lines</u>.

Unfortunately, in 1868, my wife died and I felt very lonely. I went to Canada for a while to stay with some relatives. I married my second wife, Frank Armstrong Crawford, in Ontario in 1869. I was happy again and I had many new business plans.

♦ ♦ ♦

In 1869, I bought the railway line from New York to Chicago and started to build Grand Central Depot, the station where all my railway lines ended in New York City. The station was finished in 1871. And, in 1876, I bought the Canada Southern Railway Company.

In 1873, I also gave $1 million to open a new university in Nashville in the south of the USA. It was called Vanderbilt University and it opened to students in 1875. I didn't go to university, but I wanted others to have the opportunity to study. I also wanted to help the south of the USA, which lost the Civil War. After the war, life was very difficult for people in the south of the country and I wanted to help them.

♦ ♦ ♦

When I died in 1877, I was the richest man in the USA, with a <u>fortune</u> of $100 million. I left most of my money to my son, Billy. I also left a lot of money to my wife and to my daughters.

I didn't go to university, but I learned from my experiences in business. I learned how to make good decisions and to <u>take risks</u>. And I learned to take <u>action</u> at the right time. These are the things that all good business leaders must do.

The Life of Cornelius Vanderbilt

1794   Cornelius Vanderbilt was born in Port Richmond, Staten Island, New York, USA.

1805   He left school and worked for his father's ferry business.

1810   He bought a sailing boat and started his own ferry service between Staten Island and Manhattan.

1812   He was given work by the US army to deliver goods along the Hudson River.

1813   He married Sophia Johnson. They had 13 children.

1817   Tom Gibbons asked Cornelius to become his steamship captain and business manager.

1824   Cornelius and Tom Gibbons won an important legal case against Aaron Ogden. They won the right to have a steamship business along the Hudson River.

1826   Tom Gibbons died. Cornelius continued to work for his son.

1829   Cornelius bought Tom Gibbons' ferry services.

1834	Cornelius opened The People's Line between New York and Albany. He was paid a lot of money by his competitors to close his line.
1849	The California Gold Rush started. He offered the cheapest and fastest transport for the gold back to New York.
1853	Cornelius took his family on a holiday to Europe on his steamship, *The North Star*.
1855	He opened a steamship service across the Atlantic.
1861	The Civil War started. Cornelius gave his largest ship, *The Vanderbilt*, to the Unionists.
1862	He bought the New York and Harlem Railroad.
1868	His wife died. He went to Canada to stay with relatives.
1869	He married Frank Armstrong Crawford in Canada.
1871	The Grand Central Depot railway station was opened.
1873	Cornelius gave $1 million to start a new university in Nashville, Tennessee.
1877	He died at his home at 10 Washington Place, New York City. He was 82 years old.

W. K. Kellogg

❖ ❖ ❖

1860–1951

the man who started the world's
biggest cereal company

I worked with my brother to make a breakfast cereal from <u>grain</u>. I then started my own company and <u>launched</u> Kellogg's <u>Corn</u> <u>Flakes</u>. I used <u>marketing</u> and <u>advertising</u> so Kellogg became the biggest cereal company in the world.

◆ ◆ ◆

I was born in Battle Creek, Michigan in the USA in 1860. My parents believed in good health and hard work. They started their own <u>broom</u> factory, Kellogg and Sons. My first job after I left school was to sell their brooms.

My brother, John Harvey, studied to become a doctor. In 1876, he became the director of Battle Creek Sanitarium in our home town. The Sanitarium was a sort of hospital. People went there to become healthier and live longer lives. In 1880, I started work there, too.

I looked after the accounts and became the business manager.

◆ ◆ ◆

At the Sanitarium, the patients ate only vegetables, fruits and grains. Meat wasn't allowed. My brother wanted to find a healthy new breakfast for his patients. We did experiments with different grains. In 1894, we discovered a way to make grains into flakes. We then cooked the flakes and they made a very good breakfast cereal.

The flakes became so popular with the patients that we started the Sanitas Food Company in 1897. My brother was so proud of our new breakfast cereal that he invited many people to visit our factory. They copied our idea and soon we had 42 competitors in and around Battle Creek. I was angry with my brother and I decided to start my own cereal company.

◆ ◆ ◆

In 1906, I started the Battle Creek Toasted Corn Flake Company. I decided to use corn because it grew all around the Michigan area. I wanted my corn flakes to have a name that everyone could remember. And so I launched Kellogg's Corn Flakes with my name on every box.

I also decided to add sugar to the flakes so they tasted better. My brother wasn't happy with this change. He also didn't want me to use the Kellogg name and we fought a legal case about this for many years.

My brother started his own food company. He also continued to be the director of the Sanitarium and worked on his ideas about health. I worked hard to make my cereal company a big success. I spent money on advertising. I also used new designs for the boxes and offered free <u>samples</u>. These <u>marketing</u> ideas worked and our sales grew and grew.

In 1909, we made the first 'free gift' for children. We gave a picture book to customers who bought two boxes of our corn flakes.

♦ ◆ ♦

In 1914, we started to sell our corn flakes in Canada for the first time. We were ready to open factories in Europe, but the start of the First World War stopped our plans for several years. However, we <u>created</u> some new cereals, such as Bran Flakes, and planned a new factory in Sydney, Australia.

In 1920, I finally won the <u>right</u> to use the Kellogg name. In 1922, I changed the name of my organization to the Kellogg Company and we opened a new factory in Canada. In 1927, we launched Rice Krispies which became a very popular cereal with children.

In 1929, business became more difficult for everyone. Many workers lost their jobs in the <u>Great Depression</u>. I wanted to help people, so I created many new jobs for workers in my factory. In 1930, I also started the W. K. Kellogg Foundation, which helped children from poor families.

◆ ◆ ◆

In 1938, we opened a factory in Manchester in the UK. We also <u>expanded</u> our marketing and made special radio shows for children. During the Second World War, we made special food boxes with a meal inside for the American soldiers. There was a meal in each box.

When the Second World War ended in 1945, it was wonderful news. But it was a difficult time for me. I discovered that I had glaucoma, a serious problem with my eyes. I was never able to see very well, but now I was almost <u>blind</u>. I had to slow down and not work so hard. I found some really good managers for the business and had most of my meetings with them on the phone.

In 1948, we opened a factory in South Africa. Three years later we opened a factory in Mexico. I <u>trained</u> my staff well and built a <u>successful</u> organization. I wanted my company to grow and <u>succeed</u> after I died. The corn flake was only the beginning of the story for the Kellogg Company. At the end of my long life in 1951, I wondered, 'What's next for our organization?'

The Life of W. K. Kellogg

1860   Will Keith Kellogg was born in Battle Creek, Michigan, USA.

1871   He left school and became a salesman for his parents' broom factory.

1876   His brother, Doctor John Harvey Kellogg became the director of the Battle Creek Sanitarium.

1880   W. K. Kellogg joined the Sanitarium and looked after the accounts. He was also the business manager.

1894   The Kellogg brothers discovered a way to make flakes from grains. They used it as a healthy breakfast cereal for patients at the Sanitarium.

1897   They started the Sanitas Food Company to make their cereal.

1906   W. K. Kellogg left the Sanitarium and started the Battle Creek Toasted Corn Flake Company and launched Kellogg's Corn Flakes.

1909   The company made the first 'free gift' for children. Customers who bought two boxes of Corn Flakes could get a free picture book.

1914	The company started to sell corn flakes in Canada.
1915	Bran Flakes were launched for the first time.
1922	W. K. Kellogg won the legal battle to use the Kellogg name. He changed the name of his company to the Kellogg Company. A new factory was opened in Canada.
1927	Rice Krispies were launched for the first time.
1930	The W. K. Kellogg Foundation was started. Jobs were created for workers in the Kellogg factories.
1938	The Kellogg Company opened its factory in the UK.
1939	The Second World War started. During the war, the Kellogg Company made special food boxes for soldiers.
1945	W. K. Kellogg discovered that he was almost blind.
1948	A factory was opened in South Africa.
1951	A factory was opened in Mexico. W. K. Kellogg died in Battle Creek. He was 91 years old.

Elizabeth Arden

♦♦♦

1884–1966

the woman who built the Elizabeth Arden company

I opened my first <u>salon</u> in New York City when I was 25 years old. I then <u>created</u> the Elizabeth Arden <u>brand</u> and many new beauty <u>products</u>. Elizabeth Arden became one of the most famous brands in the world.

♦ ♦ ♦

I was born in Woodbridge, Canada, in 1884. My parents gave me the name Florence Nightingale Graham. They wanted me to become a nurse like the famous British nurse, Florence Nightingale. Unfortunately, my mother died when I was 6 years old. My father did his best to look after me, but life was hard.

After I left school, I <u>trained</u> to be a nurse but I didn't like the work. I wanted to do something more exciting. In 1907, I went to live with my brother in New York City.

I was 23 years old and ready for a big new <u>opportunity</u>. I loved the bright lights of the city … and the shops!

I got my first job in a chemist's shop. I looked after the <u>accounts</u>, but I was much more interested in the shop's beauty products. They made <u>skin creams</u> in the shop and I wanted to learn all about them.

◆ ◆ ◆

I learned a lot about beauty products and soon I got a new job with Eleanor Adair in her salon. I showed the <u>clients</u> how to use skin creams and <u>cosmetics</u>. The salon was always busy. In the past, only actresses in the theatre used cosmetics. Now ordinary women wanted to use them, too. I realized that the beauty business was my big new opportunity.

In 1909, I borrowed $6,000 from my brother and started a <u>partnership</u> with a friend, Elizabeth Hubbard. In 1910, we opened the first Red Door salon. Our business was so <u>successful</u> that I was able to pay back my brother in six months. Unfortunately, the partnership with Elizabeth Hubbard didn't work and she decided to leave the business.

I was on my own, but I wasn't afraid. I wanted to build my company and sell my own cosmetics. I chose a new name for myself and my brand: Elizabeth Arden. I liked the name Elizabeth. The name Arden came from the poem 'Enoch Arden' by my favourite poet, Tennyson. I thought the name seemed very <u>elegant</u>. I wanted to create new products and so I decided to go to Paris to learn more about the beauty business.

♦ ♦ ♦

In 1912, I crossed the Atlantic and went to France. In Paris, I learned about all the new creams, cosmetics and perfumes. These products were very popular with European women. The creams and cosmetics helped women to look younger and more beautiful. And the perfumes were so elegant!

When the First World War started in 1914, I decided to return to New York. I learned so much in Paris that I was ready to create my own beauty products. I started to work with the chemist, A. Fabian Swanson. We created 'Amoretta', a face cream that was very light and easy to use. We also started to use more colour in our cosmetics for the eyes, lips and cheeks.

I worked hard on the design and <u>marketing</u> of my cosmetics. It was important that they looked elegant. My business and my brand were becoming very successful, but I was very lonely and had few friends.

Fortunately, in 1915, I got married to Thomas J. Lewis, who was an American <u>banker</u>. Thomas helped me with my business. He looked after the company accounts and gave me business advice. He believed that very rich women were the most important <u>market</u> for Elizabeth Arden products. We decided to make special <u>advertisements</u> in the most fashionable women's magazines, such as *Vogue*. This <u>advertising</u> worked really well and in 1925 the company earned more than $2 million in the USA!

♦ ◆ ♦

The <u>Great Depression</u> of 1929 was a difficult time for most businesses, but I decided to spend more money on advertising. I made the right decision because the company grew and grew during those difficult years. I created many exciting new cosmetics and opened many new salons. By 1935, there were 29 Elizabeth Arden salons around the world and 108 different products. But now there were many new <u>competitors</u> in the cosmetics business and I needed to find new opportunities.

♦ ◆ ♦

During the Second World War, I created special products for the women in the army. My bright colours for the lips, such as Montezuma Red, became very fashionable at this time. I believed in <u>high standards</u> in everything I did. I found the best managers for my business and used the best advertising. I wanted women to look and feel more beautiful so I created the best products. When women looked more beautiful, they felt wonderful, too.

I continued to work hard until the end of my life. I was very proud when Elizabeth Arden became one of the biggest brands in the world. And when I died in 1966, I wanted the new owners of my company to continue my work.

The Life of Elizabeth Arden

1884 Florence Nightingale Graham was born in Woodbridge, Ontario, Canada.

1890 Her mother died when she was 6 years old.

1907 She decided not to be a nurse and went to live with her older brother in New York City. She started work in a chemist's shop, then worked for Eleanor Adair in her salon.

1909 She started a business partnership with a friend, Elizabeth Hubbard.

1910 They opened the first Red Door salon on Fifth Avenue, New York City. Elizabeth Hubbard left the partnership. Florence changed her name to Elizabeth Arden.

1912 Elizabeth went to Paris to learn about new cosmetics.

1914 The First World War started and Elizabeth returned to New York. She created her first beauty products with A. Fabian Swanson. 'Amoretta' cream for the face was a big success.

1915 She married the American banker, Thomas J. Lewis.

1922 She opened her first salon in Paris, France.

1929	The Great Depression started. Elizabeth Arden decided to spend more money on advertising. She was successful and the company grew and grew.
1934	She started her first perfume, Blue Grass.
1935	There were 29 Elizabeth Arden salons around the world and 108 different products.
1939–1945	The Second World War. Elizabeth Arden created special products for women in the army, such as a bright red colour for the lips, Montezuma Red.
1946	She was the first woman to appear on the front cover of *Time* magazine – an important magazine in the USA.
1966	Elizabeth Arden died in New York City. She was 81 years old.

Walt Disney

❖❖❖

1901–1966

the man who started the famous
entertainment company

I started the Disney <u>animation</u> company with my brother, Roy. We <u>created</u> some of the most popular and <u>successful</u> children's films and <u>characters</u> in history. I also created the first Disneyland <u>amusement park</u> near Los Angeles, USA.

♦ ♦ ♦

I was born in Chicago, USA, in 1901, but my family soon moved to Marceline, Missouri, USA. I had three older brothers and one younger sister. We all went to school, but I was more interested in drawing than school work. When I was 7 years old, I started to sell my drawings to our neighbours.

In 1911, we moved again to Kansas City, Missouri. I became very interested in films. At that time, films were silent and in black and white. My favourite actor was Charlie Chaplin. He was very funny and sometimes I copied his way of acting for my friends.

I left home when I was 16. I wanted to join the army, but I was too young to become a soldier. Instead I became an ambulance driver and was sent to France at the end of the First World War. In France, I helped many soldiers who were hurt. It was a very sad and difficult time. I drew funny pictures on the sides of my ambulance to make everyone smile.

♦ ♦ ♦

In 1919, I was very happy to return to the USA. My brother Roy found me a job as an artist at Pesman-Rubin Art <u>Studio</u> in Kansas City. I drew pictures for newspaper and magazine <u>advertisements</u>. I met Ub Iwerks at the studio. He was also an artist and we decided to create our own <u>advertising</u> company. Unfortunately, our business wasn't successful and I had to look for a new job.

Luckily, I found work with the Kansas City Film Ad Company. I made advertisements and I became very interested in animation. I borrowed a camera and started to make short films in my free time. My first films were about a girl called Alice. A local cinema owner showed my films and they became very popular in the Kansas City area.

In 1921, after my Alice films became successful, I started a new animation company, Laugh-O-Grams. I gave jobs to Ub Iwerks and several other artists. Unfortunately, our costs became too high and I had to close the company. It was time to look for new opportunities.

• ♦ •

In 1923, I decided to move to Hollywood, Los Angeles. My brother Roy was already living there and together we started a new animation company, Disney Brothers Studio. A film distributor in New York, Margaret Winkler, ordered 12 new Alice films. We gave work to Ub Iwerks and several new artists. One of them was Lilian Bounds. I thought she was very beautiful and, in 1925, we got married. It was a happy and exciting time!

We made more Alice films for Margaret Winkler. In 1927, we also created some successful short films about *Oswald the Lucky Rabbit*. The distributor for the films was Charles Mintz for Universal Pictures. In the spring of 1928, I went to New York to ask Mintz for more money for each new Oswald film. Instead, Mintz wanted to pay us *less* per film. He also told me, 'Oswald belongs to Universal Pictures. He is our character, not yours!'

I was very angry, but I knew what to do. I needed to create a new character to compete with Oswald. And I decided that any new characters had to belong to the Disney company. The new character I created was Mickey Mouse!

• ♦ •

At first, Mickey was called Mortimer, but my wife Lilian didn't like the name. She suggested the name Mickey because it sounded more fun. Ub Iwerks designed the character and I gave Mickey his voice. In the autumn of 1928, we finished our first film with <u>sound</u>, *Steamboat Willie* and Mickey was the star! *Steamboat Willie* was a big success and Mickey Mouse became famous around the world.

The <u>Great Depression</u>, which started in 1929, made life difficult for most people. They wanted to feel happier and so they came to see our films, such as *Silly Symphonies*. In 1932, we made the first short animation in colour, *Flowers and Trees*. I won my first Academy <u>Award</u> (an Oscar®) the highest award in the film business, for this film.

♦ ♦ ♦

After Mickey Mouse, we created several other popular films and characters, including Goofy the dog in 1932 and Donald Duck in 1934. We made a lot of money from these characters and I was able to start my first <u>feature film</u> – *Snow White and the Seven Dwarfs*.

Snow White took three years and cost $1.5 million to make. Many people thought that I was crazy. My brother and my wife were very worried. They thought that the costs of the film were too high. But in the end *Snow White* was a huge success and it made $8 million in its first year!

After *Snow White*, we made many other successful feature films, including *Pinocchio*, *Dumbo* and *Bambi*. And when television became popular after the Second World

War, we made Disney TV shows. I wanted to use the money we earned from the shows to create something new and exciting … a big new amusement park, Disneyland!

♦ ♦ ♦

We started to build Disneyland in Anaheim, near Los Angeles in July 1954. I wanted to create a wonderful place that children and their parents could enjoy together. We opened Disneyland in July 1955 and soon everyone wanted to go there.

Disneyland became so successful that I bought land in Orlando, Florida to build another amusement park. Unfortunately, I didn't live to open Disneyworld in Florida. In 1965, I became very sick and my brother Roy had to continue my work. He was a fantastic business manager. He always believed in me and my dreams. I was happy for him to take Disney into the future.

Sleeping Beauty's Castle at Disneyland

The Life of Walt Disney

1901   Walter Elias Disney was born in Chicago, Illinois, USA.

1906   The Disney family moved to Marceline, Missouri.

1911   The family moved to Kansas City, Missouri.

1918   Walt became an ambulance driver at the end of the First World War.

1919   He got a job as an artist for Pesman-Rubin Art Studio in Kansas City. He started a company with Ub Iwerks, but it wasn't successful. He started to work for the Kansas City Film Ad Company and learned about animation.

1921   He started his own animation company, Laugh-O-Grams.

1923   He moved to Hollywood, Los Angeles. He started a new animation company with his brother Roy.

1925   The Disney brothers built a new studio – Walt Disney Studios. Walt married Lilian Bounds.

1927   Walt Disney Studios created *Oswald the Lucky Rabbit* for Universal Pictures.

1928	Mickey Mouse appeared for the first time in *Steamboat Willie*, the first Disney film with sound.
1932	Walt won his first Academy Award for the film *Flowers and Trees*. He also won a special Academy Award for Mickey Mouse.
1937	The first Disney feature film, *Snow White and the Seven Dwarfs*, was shown for the first time in cinemas.
1940–1942	The feature films *Pinocchio*, *Dumbo* and *Bambi* appeared in cinemas for the first time.
1950–1953	The feature films *Cinderella*, *Alice in Wonderland* and *Peter Pan* were first shown.
1954	The first Disney TV shows began.
1955	Disneyland in Anaheim, California, opened. *The Mickey Mouse Club* TV show started.
1959–64	Disney made many new feature films, including *Sleeping Beauty* and *Mary Poppins*.
1965	Land was bought in Orlando, Florida to build Disneyworld.
1966	Walt Disney died in Burbank, California. He was 65 years old.

Soichiro Honda

♦ ♦ ♦

1906–1991

the man who started the Honda motorbike
and car company

I opened a car repair business when I was 21. I then <u>manufactured</u> motorbikes and <u>created</u> the Honda company. I <u>invested</u> in <u>motor racing</u> and made cars. Honda became one of the most <u>successful</u> <u>brands</u> in the world.

◆ ◆ ◆

I was born near Hamamatsu in Japan in 1906. My father repaired bicycles. Almost everyone went to work by bicycle at that time. Only very rich people could afford cars. Every day, I helped my father in his <u>workshop</u>. I always had a dirty face from working on the bicycles and the children at school called me 'black nose'!

When I was 11 years old, I cycled 20 kilometres to see a plane for the first time. I thought it was amazing! I wanted to discover how machines worked. Maybe one day I could design and build an amazing machine?

Amazing Entrepreneurs and Business People

• ♦ •

I left school when I was 15 and went to Tokyo. I became an <u>apprentice</u> at Art Shokai, a workshop that repaired cars. At first, I cleaned the workshop and wasn't allowed to touch a car! But after a while, the workshop owner, Yuzo Sakakibara, taught me how to repair engines. I learned very quickly and Sakakibara was very pleased with my work.

Sakakibara was interested in motor racing and, in 1923, he started to make racing cars. I helped him to build the cars and, in 1924, our 'Curtiss' racing car won Japan's national race! I was only 17 and I felt very proud. Motor racing became my favourite sport.

• ♦ •

In 1928, I passed my <u>apprenticeship</u> and I opened my own <u>branch</u> of Art Shokai in Hamamatsu. Unfortunately, the <u>Great Depression</u> started in 1929 and many businesses weren't able to continue. But I worked hard and found new ways to repair cars. By 1935, I had more than 30 people working for me.

In 1935, I got married to a teacher called Isobe Sachi. We were together for 55 years and had three children. I wanted to be a success for my family so I worked really hard and demanded <u>high standards</u>. If my workers didn't do a good job, I shouted at them. They called me 'Mr <u>Thunder</u>' because of my loud voice!

I still loved motor racing and I built my own racing car, the 'Hamamatsu'. It became the fastest car in Japan. But in 1936, I had a bad accident in a race. My wife was very upset and I agreed not to race any more. I needed to concentrate on the business and to find a new business idea.

♦ ♦ ♦

In 1937, I decided to manufacture engine <u>parts</u>. I started a new company, Tokai Seiki, with a friend called Sichiro Kato. At first, we didn't do well. The quality of our engine parts wasn't good enough. I needed to learn more about metals so I studied engineering in the evenings.

Two years later, we began making engine parts for companies such as Toyota and had 2,000 people working for us. Unfortunately, our success didn't last. In 1945, at the end of the Second World War, Japan was bombed and two of our factories were destroyed. It was a terrible time.

♦ ♦ ♦

After the war, I had to rebuild my business. I thought of an exciting new idea. I added a small engine to a bicycle and created a 'motorbike'. A good friend, Takeo Fujisawa, liked my idea. He asked if he could help me with the <u>marketing</u> of my new <u>product</u>. He sent an <u>advertisement</u> to thousands of bicycle shops in Japan. The message was: 'Go faster … Save time … And enjoy the "motorbike" ride!'

'The Dream'

The advertisement was successful and we received many orders. We earned enough money from these orders to open our first factory. And in 1948, we created the Honda Motor Company. In 1949, we <u>launched</u> a motorbike called *The Dream*. It was a big success.

We were able to <u>expand</u> and manufacture new products. Soon there were Honda signs in every town and city in Japan!

♦ ◆ ♦

By the early 1960s, thousands of people were working for Honda and we started to manufacture our first cars. The Honda brand was famous in Japan, but in other countries almost nobody knew our name. It became important to expand into the international <u>market</u>. But how could we do this?

I decided to invest in Formula One – the most important motor racing <u>championship</u> in the world. In 1964, the Honda team raced for the first time in Formula One. And in 1965, we won the world championship! Suddenly, everyone knew the name Honda, and we were able to sell our cars and motorbikes around the world.

◆ ◆ ◆

In 1973, I took a big decision. I decided to leave the Honda company. I loved my work, but I wanted to spend more time on my hobbies, such as painting and travelling. Honda had many brilliant, young managers. It was their turn to decide the future of Honda. I made a good decision. In the last years of my life it was wonderful to see the company change and grow. When I died in 1991, Honda was one of the biggest car companies in the world.

The Life of Soichiro Honda

1906	Soichiro Honda was born near Hamamatsu, Japan.
1917	He cycled 20 kilometres to see a plane for the first time. He became very interested in how machines work.
1922	He left school and went to Tokyo when he was 15 years old.
1922–1928	He worked as an apprentice at Art Shokai, a workshop that repaired cars. He helped the owner, Yuzo Sakakibara, to build a racing car called the 'Curtiss'. The car won the national motor race in 1924.
1928	Soichiro returned home to Hamamatsu and opened his own branch of Art Shokai.
1935	He got married to Isobe Sachi, a school teacher.
1936	He had a bad accident in his own racing car, the 'Hamamatsu'. He decided not to race any more.
1937	He started the company, Tokai Seiki with a friend, Sichiro Kato. Soichiro studied engineering for two years in the evenings. Tokai Seiki manufactured engine parts for Toyota and other companies.

1945   Two of Tokai Seiki's factories were destroyed at the end of the Second World War.

1946   Soichiro designed a bicycle with a small engine. Takeo Fujisawa helped Soichiro to market his 'motorbike'.

1948   Soichiro started the Honda Motor Company.

1949   The successful motorbike, *The Dream*, was launched by the Honda Motor Company.

1963   Honda started to manufacture cars for the first time.

1964   Honda entered Formula One for the first time.

1965   Honda won the Formula One championship.

1973   Soichiro left the Honda company to spend more time on his hobbies. He continued to give advice to the company.

1991   He died in Tokyo, Japan. He was 84 years old.

◆ Glossary ◆

accounts PLURAL NOUN
records of all the money that a person or a business receives and spends

action UNCOUNTABLE NOUN
something that you do for a particular purpose

advertisement NOUN
information in a newspaper or magazine that tells you about a product, and tries to make you buy it

advertising UNCOUNTABLE NOUN
the business of creating information about products to try to make you buy them

amusement park NOUN
a place where people pay to ride on machines for fun

animation NOUN
a film which does not show real people but which has drawings that appear to move

apprentice NOUN
a young person who works for someone in order to learn their skill

apprenticeship NOUN
a period of time when a young person works for an expert in order to learn a skill

award NOUN
a prize that is given to someone because they did something well

banker NOUN
someone who works for a bank at a senior level

banking UNCOUNTABLE NOUN
the business activity that banks do

blind ADJECTIVE
not able to see

branch NOUN
one of the offices or shops that form part of a bigger company

brand NOUN
the name of a product that a particular company makes

broom NOUN
a type of brush with a long handle used for sweeping the floor

championship NOUN
a competition to find the best player or team in a particular sport or game

Glossary

character NOUN
one of the people in a story

civil war NOUN
a war between different groups of people who live in the same country

client NOUN
a person who pays someone for a service

compete VERB
to try and make people buy the products that you are selling, rather than products from another company

competitor NOUN
a company that is trying to sell the same sort of products as you are

corn UNCOUNTABLE NOUN
the yellow seeds of a plant that is a type of tall grass. **Corn** is used for food

cosmetics PLURAL NOUN
products that women use on their faces to make themselves look more beautiful

create VERB
to make something happen or exist

currency exchange UNCOUNTABLE NOUN
changing money, such as American dollars, into another sort of money, such as British pounds

distributor NOUN
a company that sends films from the film makers to cinemas all over the country

elegant ADJECTIVE
beautiful in a simple way

emperor NOUN
a man who rules a group of countries (= an empire)

empire NOUN
a group of countries who are ruled by a single powerful country

expand VERB
1 to make something such as a company or an empire become bigger
2 to become bigger

feature film NOUN
a long film that tells a story and is shown in cinemas

ferry NOUN
a boat that regularly takes people or things a short distance across water

flake NOUN
a small thin and flat piece of something

fortune NOUN
a very large amount of money

Gold Rush NOUN
the time when a lot of people suddenly went to California because gold had been discovered there

grain NOUN
a single seed from a particular plant. **Grains** are used for food

Great Depression NOUN
a period of time that started in 1929 and lasted several years, when lots of companies had to stop working and lots of workers lost their jobs

high standards NOUN
the best quality that is possible in a particular product or activity

invest VERB
to give money to a business or a bank, because you hope they will give you back more money than you gave them

investment NOUN
money that you give to a company or bank in order to get a bigger amount of money in return

launch VERB
to start to sell a new product

legal case NOUN
a process during which a judge makes a decision about whether something is right or wrong

line NOUN
1 a company that owns trains or ships that regularly carry people and goods along particular routes

2 a route that trains move along

manufacture VERB
to make something in a factory

market VERB
to organize the way a product is sold by arranging advertising and deciding where exactly to sell it
NOUN
all the places where a product can be sold, and all the people who might buy it

marketing UNCOUNTABLE NOUN
the organization of the way a product is sold

monopoly NOUN
a situation where a particular type of product is being sold by only one company, with the result that they can charge high prices

Glossary

motor racing NOUN
the sport of driving cars very fast in a race to see who is the fastest driver

opportunity NOUN
a situation in which it is possible for you to do something that you want to do

part NOUN
a piece of a machine

partnership NOUN
when two or more people share control of a company

patient NOUN
a person who receives medical treatment from a doctor

powerful ADJECTIVE
able to control people and events

product NOUN
something that you make or grow in order to sell it

right NOUN
permission that you have to do something because the law says you can do it

risk
to take a risk PHRASE
to do something that will be good for you if it works, but which will have very bad results if it does not work

salon NOUN
a place where you go to have your hair cut, or to have beauty treatments

sample NOUN
a small amount of something which people can try, and if they like it they can buy some more

service NOUN
1 a job that an organization or business can do for you
2 something that the public needs, such as transport or energy supplies

shareholder NOUN
a person who owns shares (= parts of a company's value)

skin cream UNCOUNTABLE NOUN
a very thick liquid that you can put on your face or skin to make your skin soft and healthy

sound NOUN
the actors' words and the music and other noises that you can hear when you are watching a film

steamship NOUN
a ship that gets its power from steam

Amazing Entrepreneurs and Business People

studio NOUN
a building or room where actors are filmed to make a film or television programme

succeed VERB
to get the result that you wanted

successful ADJECTIVE
managing to do what you want to do and getting the results you wanted

survive VERB
to continue to exist after a difficult or dangerous time

thunder UNCOUNTABLE NOUN
the loud noise that you sometimes hear from the sky during a storm

train VERB
1 to teach people the skills that they need in order to do something

2 to learn the skills that you need in order to do something

workshop NOUN
a place where people make or repair things